2005

JANUARY

S	M	T	W	T	F	S
						1
2	3	4	5	6	7	8
9	10	11	12	13	14	15
16	17	18	19	20	21	22
23	24	25	26	27	28	29
30	31					

FEBRUARY

S	M	T	W	T	F	S
		1	2	3	4	5
6	7	8	9	10	11	12
13	14	15	16	17	18	19
20	21	22	23	24	25	26
27	28					

MARCH

S	M	T	W	T	F	S
		1	2	3	4	5
6	7	8	9	10	11	12
13	14	15	16	17	18	19
20	21	22	23	24	25	26
27	28	29	30	31		

APRIL

S	M	T	W	T	F	S
					1	2
3	4	5	6	7	8	9
10	11	12	13	14	15	16
17	18	19	20	21	22	23
24	25	26	27	28	29	30

MAY

S	M	T	W	T	F	S
1	2	3	4	5	6	7
8	9	10	11	12	13	14
15	16	17	18	19	20	21
22	23	24	25	26	27	28
29	30	31				

JUNE

S	M	T	W	T	F	S
			1	2	3	4
5	6	7	8	9	10	11
12	13	14	15	16	17	18
19	20	21	22	23	24	25
26	27	28	29	30		

JULY

S	M	T	W	T	F	S
					1	2
3	4	5	6	7	8	9
10	11	12	13	14	15	16
17	18	19	20	21	22	23
24	25	26	27	28	29	30
31						

AUGUST

S	M	T	W	T	F	S
	1	2	3	4	5	6
7	8	9	10	11	12	13
14	15	16	17	18	19	20
21	22	23	24	25	26	27
28	29	30	31			

SEPTEMBER

S	M	T	W	T	F	S
				1	2	3
4	5	6	7	8	9	10
11	12	13	14	15	16	17
18	19	20	21	22	23	24
25	26	27	28	29	30	

OCTOBER

S	M	T	W	T	F	S
						1
2	3	4	5	6	7	8
9	10	11	12	13	14	15
16	17	18	19	20	21	22
23	24	25	26	27	28	29
30	31					

NOVEMBER

S	M	T	W	T	F	S
		1	2	3	4	5
6	7	8	9	10	11	12
13	14	15	16	17	18	19
20	21	22	23	24	25	26
27	28	29	30			

DECEMBER

S	M	T	W	T	F	S
				1	2	3
4	5	6	7	8	9	10
11	12	13	14	15	16	17
18	19	20	21	22	23	24
25	26	27	28	29	30	31

PERSONAL NOTES

NAME ....

ADDRESS ....

....

....

....

TELEPHONE (PRIVATE) ....

TELEPHONE (BUSINESS) ....

TELEPHONE (MOBILE) ....

FAX ....

EMAIL ....

NOTES ....

....

....

....

....

If this Diary is found, please return to the owner at the above address

TOLKIEN

The Lord of the Rings

5oth Anniversary Diary

ILLUSTRATED BY

J.R.R. TOLKIEN

HarperCollins*Publishers*

HarperCollins*Publishers*
77-85 Fulham Palace Road
Hammersmith
London W6 8JB
www.tolkien.co.uk

Published by HarperCollins*Publishers* 2004
The Tolkien Diary 2005
© HarperCollins*Publishers* 2004

All text extracts have been adapted from *J.R.R. Tolkien: Artist & Illustrator* by Wayne G. Hammond & Christina Scull. This book explores Tolkien's art at length, from his childhood paintings to his final sketches, and includes 200 reproductions. At its heart are his illustrations for his books, especially his tales of Middle-earth: *The Silmarillion*, *The Hobbit* and *The Lord of the Rings*.

The images in this diary are reproduced courtesy of the Bodleian Library, University of Oxford, from their holdings: MS Tolkien Drawings 71; 72; 73; 74; 75; 76r; 76v; 79; 80; 81; 89, fol. 12r; 89, fol. 14; 89, fol. 15; 90, fol. 13; 90, fol. 18; 90, fol. 21; 90, fol. 29; 90, fol. 30 and 98, fol. 1.

 ® and Tolkien® are registered trade marks of The J.R.R. Tolkien Estate Limited

ISBN 0 00 717403 9

Printed and bound in Singapore for Imago

WORKS BY J.R.R. TOLKIEN

THE HOBBIT
LEAF BY NIGGLE
ON FAIRY-STORIES
FARMER GILES OF HAM
THE HOMECOMING OF BEORHTNOTH
THE LORD OF THE RINGS
THE ADVENTURES OF TOM BOMBADIL
THE ROAD GOES EVER ON (WITH DONALD SWANN)
SMITH OF WOOTTON MAJOR

WORKS PUBLISHED POSTHUMOUSLY

SIR GAWAIN AND THE GREEN KNIGHT, PEARL
    AND SIR ORFEO
THE FATHER CHRISTMAS LETTERS
THE SILMARILLION
PICTURES BY J.R.R. TOLKIEN
UNFINISHED TALES
THE LETTERS OF J.R.R. TOLKIEN
FINN AND HENGEST
MR BLISS
THE MONSTERS AND THE CRITICS & OTHER ESSAYS
ROVERANDOM

THE HISTORY OF MIDDLE-EARTH

BY CHRISTOPHER TOLKIEN
I THE BOOK OF LOST TALES, PART ONE
II THE BOOK OF LOST TALES, PART TWO
III THE LAYS OF BELERIAND
IV THE SHAPING OF MIDDLE-EARTH
V THE LOST ROAD AND OTHER WRITINGS
VI THE RETURN OF THE SHADOW
VII THE TREASON OF ISENGARD
VIII THE WAR OF THE RING
IX SAURON DEFEATED
X MORGOTH'S RING
XI THE WAR OF THE JEWELS
XII THE PEOPLES OF MIDDLE-EARTH

THE LORD OF THE RINGS

J.R.R. TOLKIEN began writing *The Lord of the Rings* between 16 and 19 December 1937. *The Hobbit*, published three months earlier, was an immediate success, and Tolkien's publishers, George Allen & Unwin, were encouraging him (against his inclination) to write a sequel. He could not think of anything more to say about hobbits; he had remarked to Stanley Unwin in a letter of 15 October 1937: 'Mr Baggins seems to have exhibited so fully both the Took and the Baggins sides of their nature… But if it is true that *The Hobbit* has come to stay and more will be wanted, I will start the process of thought, and try to get some idea of a theme drawn from this material suitable for treatment in a similar style and for a similar audience – possibly including actual hobbits.'

In the face of Unwin's continued lack of enthusiasm for publishing *The Silmarillion*, Tolkien later wrote to him: 'I think it is plain that… a sequel or successor to *The Hobbit* is called for. But I am sure you will sympathize when I say that the construction of elaborate and consistent mythology (and two languages) rather occupies the mind, and the Silmarils are in my heart. So that goodness knows what will happen.' Three days later, he wrote to C.A. Furth at Allen & Unwin: 'I have written the first chapter of a new story about Hobbits – "A long expected party".'

The history of the writing of *The Lord of the Rings* is told in detail by Christopher Tolkien in four volumes of his *History of Middle-earth* series: *The Return of the Shadow*, *The Treason of Isengard*, *The War of the Ring* and *Sauron Defeated*. A brief summary of this history is contained in *J.R.R. Tolkien: A Descriptive Bibliography* by Wayne G. Hammond, with the assistance of Douglas A. Anderson. Here, however, it will suffice to say that the work was often delayed by Tolkien's duties at Oxford, by the Second World War, by ill health, by bouts of failed inspiration, and by the distraction of other writings. Tolkien did not finish writing it until 1949.

As Tolkien remarked in the foreword to its second edition, *The Lord of the Rings* 'grew in the telling' until it was not simply another story about hobbits, but part of the larger mythology that was in his heart. He came to feel that *The Lord of the Rings* was the 'continuation and completion' of *The Silmarillion*, and that the two works should be published 'in conjunction or connexion'. Allen & Unwin, however, could not afford to publish both works as the author wished, nor could Collins, with whom Tolkien dealt in 1949-52. The works were enormous, and production costs were rising, but with the arrival of Rayner Unwin at his father's firm Tolkien at last received encouraging word on his 'great (though not flawless) work', as he called it in a letter to Unwin, and it was eventually agreed that Allen & Unwin would publish *The Lord of the Rings* in three volumes. After a long and difficult period of production, *The Fellowship of the Ring* was published on 21st July 1954. *The Two Towers* followed this on 11th November, and *The Return of the King* finally appeared on 20th October 1955, it having taken almost a year to bring the appendices, which Tolkien considered essential to the work, to a satisfactory conclusion.

J.R.R. TOLKIEN

JOHN RONALD REUEL TOLKIEN was born on 3rd January 1892 in Bloemfontein in the Orange Free State.

In early 1895, exhausted by the climate, his mother, Mabel, returned to England with Ronald and his younger brother, Hilary. After his father's death from rheumatic fever, he and his family settled briefly at Sarehole, near Birmingham. This beautiful rural area made a great impression on the young Ronald, and its effect can clearly be seen in his later writing and in some of his pictures.

Mabel died in 1904, leaving the boys in the care of Father Francis Morgan, a priest at the Birmingham Oratory. At King Edward's School, Birmingham, Ronald developed his love of languages; later he invented languages of his own. Also at this time he met Edith Bratt, whom he married in 1916.

At the outbreak of the First World War in 1914, Ronald was still a student at Oxford. He graduated the following year with a First in English, and soon afterward took up a commission as a second lieutenant in the Lancashire Fusiliers. In 1916 he fought in the Battle of the Somme, but was struck down by trench fever and invalided home.

One of the finest philologists of his day, Tolkien spent most of his working life at Oxford, first as Professor of Anglo-Saxon and then Professor of English Language and Literature. At the same time, in private, he worked on the great cycle of myths and legends later published as THE SILMARILLION. He and Edith had four children, and it was partly for them that he wrote the tale of THE HOBBIT, first published in 1937 by George Allen & Unwin. This was so successful that the publisher immediately wanted a sequel, but it was not until 1954 that the first volume of Tolkien's masterpiece, THE LORD OF THE RINGS, was published to instant acclaim. Its enormous popularity took Tolkien by surprise.

Later in life Ronald and Edith Tolkien moved to Bournemouth, but when Edith died in 1971 Tolkien returned to Oxford. He himself died after a brief illness on 2nd September 1973.

2005

BRANDYWINE FERRY

Pencil, coloured pencil

J.R.R. Tolkien drew or painted most of his illustrations for *The Hobbit* after its text was complete, when it was to be published or reprinted. In contrast, his pictures for *The Lord of the Rings* were drawn while that work was being written, and for the most part are quick, rough sketches made in aid of the writing.

One of the earliest of these, and one of unfortunately very few pictures Tolkien made of the Hobbit lands in Middle-earth, depicts the Bucklebury ferry over the river Brandywine, from a scene in Book I, Chapter 5, in which Frodo and his companions are travelling east to Crickhollow. Like the rest of the *Lord of the Rings* art the sketch bears no written date, but it clearly post-dates the earliest text. The hobbit holding the pole is also sketched separately, very small, at the top of the sheet. This drawing was the last, among all of Tolkien's extant art, in which he drew the human figure.

January

OLD MAN WILLOW

Pencil, coloured pencil

On occasion Tolkien made more finished drawings for *The Lord of the Rings*, for his own pleasure as well as for reference in writing. *Old Man Willow* is a fine example. It illustrates the deceptively tranquil scene the hobbits come upon suddenly out of the gloom of the Old Forest in Book I, Chapter 6, dominated by a huge willow-tree: 'Enormous it looked, its sprawling branches going up like reaching arms with many long-fingered hands, its knotted and twisted trunk gaping in wide fissures that creaked faintly as the boughs moved.' With a little imagination one can see a 'face' on the upper right part of the trunk.

Old Man Willow

December 2004

MONDAY 20	TUESDAY 21	WEDNESDAY 22	THURSDAY 23

FRIDAY 24

SATURDAY 25
Christmas Day

SUNDAY 26
Boxing Day
St. Stephen's Day [ROI]
Day of Good Will [SA]

Weeks 0-1

DECEMBER

S	M	T	W	T	F	S
			1	2	3	4
5	6	7	8	9	10	11
12	13	14	15	16	17	18
19	20	21	22	23	24	25
26	27	28	29	30	31	

January 2005

MONDAY 27

TUESDAY 28

WEDNESDAY 29

THURSDAY 30

FRIDAY 31

SATURDAY 1

New Year's Day

SUNDAY 2

JANUARY

S	M	T	W	T	F	S
						1
2	3	4	5	6	7	8
9	10	11	12	13	14	15
16	17	18	19	20	21	22
23	24	25	26	27	28	29
30	31					

January

MONDAY 3

New Year's Day
[holiday in lieu] [UK & ROI]
J.R.R. Tolkien born, 1892
Last Quarter ◗

TUESDAY 4

WEDNESDAY 5

THURSDAY 6

Epiphany

Weeks 2-3

FRIDAY 7

SATURDAY 8

SUNDAY 9

JANUARY

S	M	T	W	T	F	S
						1
2	3	4	5	6	7	8
9	10	11	12	13	14	15
16	17	18	19	20	21	22
23	24	25	26	27	28	29
30	31					

MONDAY 10

New Moon ●

TUESDAY 11

On this day S.R. 1419 the Fellowship were caught in snow on Caradhras.

WEDNESDAY 12

THURSDAY 13

FRIDAY 14

SATURDAY 15

SUNDAY 16

JANUARY

S	M	T	W	T	F	S
						1
2	3	4	5	6	7	8
9	10	11	12	13	14	15
16	17	18	19	20	21	22
23	24	25	26	27	28	29
30	31					

# January

MONDAY 17

Martin Luther King, Jnr. Day [USA]
First Quarter ◐

On this day S.R.1419 the company came
to Caras Galadhon at evening.

···

Weeks 4-5

TUESDAY 18

WEDNESDAY 19

THURSDAY 20

Inauguration Day [USA]

FRIDAY 21

Eid-al-Adha

SATURDAY 22

SUNDAY 23

JANUARY

S	M	T	W	T	F	S
						1
2	3	4	5	6	7	8
9	10	11	12	13	14	15
16	17	18	19	20	21	22
23	24	25	26	27	28	29
30	31					

On this day S.R.1419 Gandalf pursued
the Balrog to the peak of Zirakzigil.

January

MONDAY 24

TUESDAY 25
Full Moon ○

WEDNESDAY 26
Australia Day [Aus]

THURSDAY 27

FRIDAY 28

SATURDAY 29

SUNDAY 30

In a letter to his son Christopher dated 30th January 1945 J.R.R. Tolkien wrote:

'*The first War of the Machines seems to be drawing to its final inconclusive chapter - leaving, alas, everyone the poorer, many bereaved or maimed and millions dead, and only one thing triumphant: the Machines.*'

| **JANUARY** | | | | | | |
S	M	T	W	T	F	S
						1
2	3	4	5	6	7	8
9	10	11	12	13	14	15
16	17	18	19	20	21	22
23	24	25	26	27	28	29
30	31					

February

RIVENDELL LOOKING EAST

Pencil, coloured pencil

Although drawn probably in the 1930s, while Tolkien was still at work on *The Hobbit*, this virtuoso work serves as well as an illustration for *The Lord of the Rings*. The valley appears quite deep, with the surrounding mountain walls rising to great heights and Elrond's house partly hidden by trees. In this Tolkien used at least seven different colours as well as grey; its variety of textures were built up chiefly with lines made with the pencil point, closer to some of Tolkien's 'Silmarillion' art of the 1920s than to the blended shading that he came to prefer in the following decade.

Rivendell.
looking East

January

MONDAY 31

Weeks 6-7

TUESDAY 1

WEDNESDAY 2

Last Quarter ◑

From a letter to his publisher dated 2nd February 1939:

'I think The Lord of the Rings is in itself a good deal better than The Hobbit, but it may not prove to be a very fit sequel. It is more grown-up… The readers who clamoured for "more about the Necromancer" are to blame, for the N. is not child's play.'

THURSDAY 3

FRIDAY 4

SATURDAY 5

SUNDAY 6

Waitangi Day [NZ]

JANUARY

S	M	T	W	T	F	S
						1
2	3	4	5	6	7	8
9	10	11	12	13	14	15
16	17	18	19	20	21	22
23	24	25	26	27	28	29
30	31					

February

MONDAY 7

TUESDAY 8

Chinese New Year
Shrove Tuesday
New Moon ●

WEDNESDAY 9

Ash Wednesday

THURSDAY 10

Islamic New Year (AH1426)

FRIDAY 11

SATURDAY 12

Lincoln's Birthday [USA]

SUNDAY 13

'One Ring to rule them all,
One Ring to find them,
One Ring to bring them all and
in the Darkness bind them.'

FEBRUARY

S	M	T	W	T	F	S
		1	2	3	4	5
6	7	8	9	10	11	12
13	14	15	16	17	18	19
20	21	22	23	24	25	26
27	28					

February

MONDAY 14

St Valentine's Day

Weeks 8-9

TUESDAY 15

WEDNESDAY 16

First Quarter ◖

THURSDAY 17

On this day S.R. 1419 Gwaihir bore Gandalf from Zirakzigil to Lórien.

FRIDAY 18

SATURDAY 19

SUNDAY 20

FEBRUARY

S	M	T	W	T	F	S
		1	2	3	4	5
6	7	8	9	10	11	12
13	14	15	16	17	18	19
20	21	22	23	24	25	26
27	28					

February

MONDAY 21

Presidents' Day [USA]

TUESDAY 22

Washington's Birthday [USA]

WEDNESDAY 23

THURSDAY 24

Full Moon ○

FRIDAY 25

SATURDAY 26

SUNDAY 27

This day, S.R. 1419, marks the Breaking of the Fellowship and the departure of Boromir.

FEBRUARY

S	M	T	W	T	F	S
		1	2	3	4	5
6	7	8	9	10	11	12
13	14	15	16	17	18	19
20	21	22	23	24	25	26
27	28					

March

MORIA GATE

Pencil, coloured pencil

Tolkien drew this view of the West Gate of Moria, originally a single picture, probably before he had written Book II, Chapter 4 of *The Lord of the Rings* in which the Fellowship approach the entrance to the Mines: 'Rounding the corner they saw before them a low cliff, some five fathoms high, with a broken and jagged top. Over it a trickling water dripped. . . .' Realizing that the Stair Falls as drawn are hardly trickling or dripping, Tolkien removed the lower portion of the picture and kept its more accurate upper part. He wrote the title of the work only roughly in the larger piece, while in the true bottom the title appears elegantly within a panel that echoes the twisting pillars of Moria Gate between the two trees.

February

MONDAY 28

TUESDAY 1

St. David's Day [Wales]

WEDNESDAY 2

THURSDAY 3

Last Quarter ◑

Weeks 10-11

FRIDAY 4

SATURDAY 5

SUNDAY 6

Mothering Sunday

FEBRUARY

S	M	T	W	T	F	S
		1	2	3	4	5
6	7	8	9	10	11	12
13	14	15	16	17	18	19
20	21	22	23	24	25	26
27	28					

March

MONDAY 7

TUESDAY 8

On this day S.R. 1419 Aragorn took the 'Paths of the Dead' at daybreak, reaching Erech at midnight.

WEDNESDAY 9

THURSDAY 10

New Moon ●

'*When evening in the Shire*
was grey
his footsteps on the Hill
were heard;
before the dawn he went away
on journey long without a word.'
Frodo's Lament for Gandalf

FRIDAY 11

SATURDAY 12

On this day, S.R. 1419, Gollum led Frodo into Shelob's Lair.

SUNDAY 13

On 13th March S.R. 1419 Frodo was captured by the Orcs of Cirith Ungol.

MARCH

S	M	T	W	T	F	S
			1	2	3	4	5
6	7	8	9	10	11	12
13	14	15	16	17	18	19
20	21	22	23	24	25	26
27	28	29	30	31		

# March

MONDAY 14
Commonwealth Day

TUESDAY 15
Canberra Day [Aus]

WEDNESDAY 16

THURSDAY 17
St. Patrick's Day [Ireland]
First Quarter ◑

Weeks 12-13

FRIDAY 18

SATURDAY 19

SUNDAY 20
Vernal Equinox
Palm Sunday

MARCH

S	M	T	W	T	F	S
		1	2	3	4	5
6	7	8	9	10	11	12
13	14	15	16	17	18	19
20	21	22	23	24	25	26
27	28	29	30	31		

On 19th March S.R. 1419 the Host came to the Morgul-vale. Sam and Frodo escaped the Tower of Cirith Ungol and began their journey along the road to Barad-dûr.

March

MONDAY 21

Human Rights Day [South Africa]

TUESDAY 22

Indian New Year [Saka]

WEDNESDAY 23

THURSDAY 24

FRIDAY 25

Good Friday
Full Moon ○

SATURDAY 26

SUNDAY 27

Easter Day
British Summer Time begins

On 25th March S.R. 1421 Elanor the Fair,
daughter of Samwise and Rosie, was born.

MARCH

S	M	T	W	T	F	S
		1	2	3	4	5
6	7	8	9	10	11	12
13	14	15	16	17	18	19
20	21	22	23	24	25	26
27	28	29	30	31		

April

THE FOREST OF LOTHLORIEN IN SPRING

Pencil, coloured pencil

This fine example of Tolkien's mature coloured pencil technique, drawn probably in the early 1940s, actually depicts the mallorn trees of Lothlórien as described by Legolas in Book II, Chapter 6 of *The Lord of the Rings*, rather than the forest as seen by the Fellowship in winter: 'Not till the spring comes and the new green opens do [the leaves] fall, and then the boughs are laden with yellow flowers; and the floor of the wood is golden, and golden is the roof, and its pillars are of silver, for the bark of the trees is smooth and grey.'

The Forest of Lothlorien in Spring

# March

MONDAY 28

Easter Monday [UK & ROI]

On 28th March S.R. 1419 Celeborn crossed the Anduin.

....

Weeks 14-15

TUESDAY 29

WEDNESDAY 30

THURSDAY 31

FRIDAY 1

SATURDAY 2

Last Quarter ◖

SUNDAY 3

Daylight Saving Time begins [USA]

MARCH

S	M	T	W	T	F	S
		1	2	3	4	5
6	7	8	9	10	11	12
13	14	15	16	17	18	19
20	21	22	23	24	25	26
27	28	29	30	31		

April

MONDAY 4

TUESDAY 5

WEDNESDAY 6

THURSDAY 7

On 6th April S.R. 1419 the Ring-bearers were honoured on the Field of Cormallen.

FRIDAY 8

New Moon ●

SATURDAY 9

SUNDAY 10

'Old Tom Bombadil was a
merry fellow;
bright blue his jacket was
and his boots were yellow,
green were his girdle
and his breeches all of leather;
he wore in his tall hat
a swan-wing feather.'

APRIL

S	M	T	W	T	F	S
					1	2
3	4	5	6	7	8	9
10	11	12	13	14	15	16
17	18	19	20	21	22	23
24	25	26	27	28	29	30

 April

MONDAY 11

TUESDAY 12

Family Day [South Africa]

WEDNESDAY 13

THURSDAY 14

From a letter to Christopher Tolkien dated 14th April 1944:

'I managed to get an hour or two's writing and have brought Frodo nearly to the gates of Mordor…'

Weeks 16-17

FRIDAY 15

SATURDAY 16

First Quarter ◗

SUNDAY 17

APRIL

S	M	T	W	T	F	S
					1	2
3	4	5	6	7	8	9
10	11	12	13	14	15	16
17	18	19	20	21	22	23
24	25	26	27	28	29	30

April

MONDAY 18	TUESDAY 19	WEDNESDAY 20	THURSDAY 21

FRIDAY 22	SATURDAY 23	SUNDAY 24	
	St. George's Day [England]	First Day of Passover Full Moon ○	

APRIL

S	M	T	W	T	F	S
					1	2
3	4	5	6	7	8	9
10	11	12	13	14	15	16
17	18	19	20	21	22	23
24	25	26	27	28	29	30

May

FANGORN FOREST (TAUR-NA-FÚIN)

Pencil, black ink, watercolour

This image, in different forms, was used to illustrate all three of Tolkien's major works. *Taur-na-Fúin*, painted in July 1928, depicts the elves Beleg and Gwindor in the 'Silmarillion' tale of Túrin. Redrawn in ink as *Mirkwood*, it was included in early printings of *The Hobbit*. And when the original watercolour was published in the *J.R.R. Tolkien Calendar 1974*, it was as an illustration for *The Lord of the Rings*. Tolkien seems to have felt that his 'Silmarillion' picture could do double duty with a simple change of title; but its slender figures, one with pointed red shoes, are clearly elves, not the hobbits Merry and Pippin in Fangorn Forest.

April

MONDAY 25

Anzac Day [Aus/NZ]

TUESDAY 26

WEDNESDAY 27

Freedom Day [South Africa]

THURSDAY 28

Weeks 18-19

FRIDAY 29

SATURDAY 30

SUNDAY 1

Worker's Day [South Africa]
Last Quarter ☽

APRIL

S	M	T	W	T	F	S
					1	2
3	4	5	6	7	8	9
10	11	12	13	14	15	16
17	18	19	20	21	22	23
24	25	26	27	28	29	30

On 1st May S.R. 1420 Master Samwise married Rosie Cotton.

May

MONDAY 2
Early May Bank Holiday [UK & ROI]

TUESDAY 3

WEDNESDAY 4

THURSDAY 5

FRIDAY 6

SATURDAY 7

SUNDAY 8
Mother's Day [USA/Can/Aus/NZ/SA]
New Moon ●

'O Elbereth! Gilthoniel!
We still remember, we who dwell
In this far land beneath the trees,
Thy starlight on the Western
*   Seas.'*

From a letter to Christopher Tolkien
dated 6th May 1944:

'A new character has come on the scene (I
am sure I did not invent him, I did not
even want him, though I like him, but
there he came, walking out of the woods of
Ithilien): Faramir, the brother of Boromir.'

MAY

S	M	T	W	T	F	S
1	2	3	4	5	6	7
8	9	10	11	12	13	14
15	16	17	18	19	20	21
22	23	24	25	26	27	28
29	30	31				

May

MONDAY 9

TUESDAY 10

WEDNESDAY 11

THURSDAY 12

Weeks 20-21

FRIDAY 13

SATURDAY 14

SUNDAY 15

Whit Sunday

MAY

S	M	T	W	T	F	S
1	2	3	4	5	6	7
8	9	10	11	12	13	14
15	16	17	18	19	20	21
22	23	24	25	26	27	28
29	30	31				

May

MONDAY 16

First Quarter ◗

TUESDAY 17

WEDNESDAY 18

THURSDAY 19

FRIDAY 20

SATURDAY 21

SUNDAY 22

From a letter to Christopher Tolkien dated 21st May 1944:

'Do you think SHELOB is a good name for a monstrous spider figure? It is of course only "she+lob" (=spider), but written as one, it seems to be quite noisome.'

MAY

S	M	T	W	T	F	S
1	2	3	4	5	6	7
8	9	10	11	12	13	14
15	16	17	18	19	20	21
22	23	24	25	26	27	28
29	30	31				

May

MONDAY 23

Victoria Day [Can]
Full Moon ○

Weeks 22-23

TUESDAY 24

WEDNESDAY 25

THURSDAY 26

FRIDAY 27

SATURDAY 28

SUNDAY 29

MAY

S	M	T	W	T	F	S
1	2	3	4	5	6	7
8	9	10	11	12	13	14
15	16	17	18	19	20	21
22	23	24	25	26	27	28
29	30	31				

June

MONDAY 30

Spring Bank Holiday [UK]
Memorial Day [US]
Last Quarter ◐

TUESDAY 31

WEDNESDAY 1

THURSDAY 2

FRIDAY 3

SATURDAY 4

SUNDAY 5

'Gondor! Gondor, between the
Mountains and the Sea!
West Wind blew there;
the light upon the Silver Tree
Fell like bright rain in the
gardens of the Kings of old.'

JUNE

S	M	T	W	T	F	S
			1	2	3	4
5	6	7	8	9	10	11
12	13	14	15	16	17	18
19	20	21	22	23	24	25
26	27	28	29	30		

June

HELM'S DEEP & THE HORNBURG

Pencil, coloured pencil

The geography of Helm's Deep in the land of Rohan required careful planning. In preparation for the fierce battle fought there in Book III, Chapter 7 of *The Lord of the Rings*, Tolkien drew this picture on a discarded leaf of examination paper. It provides a close look at the fortress and the Deeping Wall and a splendid perspective view of the gorge with the three peaks of Tindtorras (Thrihyrne) in the distance. The Deeping-stream snakes around the causeway and out through a gap in a curved line at the bottom of the drawing, which is surely meant to indicate Helm's Dike.

 # June

MONDAY 6

Holiday [ROI]
Queen's Birthday [NZ]
New Moon ●

Weeks 24-25

TUESDAY 7

WEDNESDAY 8

THURSDAY 9

FRIDAY 10

SATURDAY 11

SUNDAY 12

JUNE

S	M	T	W	T	F	S
			1	2	3	4
5	6	7	8	9	10	11
12	13	14	15	16	17	18
19	20	21	22	23	24	25
26	27	28	29	30		

June

MONDAY 13
Queen's Birthday [Aus]

TUESDAY 14

On 14th June S.R. 1419 the sons of Elrond met Arwen's escort and brought her to Edoras.

WEDNESDAY 15
First Quarter ◑

THURSDAY 16
Youth Day [South Africa]

FRIDAY 17

SATURDAY 18

SUNDAY 19
Father's Day [UK & USA]

J U N E						
S	M	T	W	T	F	S
			1	2	3	4
5	6	7	8	9	10	11
12	13	14	15	16	17	18
19	20	21	22	23	24	25
26	27	28	29	30		

June

MONDAY 20

TUESDAY 21

Summer Solstice

WEDNESDAY 22

Full Moon ○

THURSDAY 23

Weeks 26-27

FRIDAY 24

SATURDAY 25

SUNDAY 26

JUNE

S	M	T	W	T	F	S
			1	2	3	4
5	6	7	8	9	10	11
12	13	14	15	16	17	18
19	20	21	22	23	24	25
26	27	28	29	30		

July

MONDAY 27

TUESDAY 28

Last Quarter ◖

WEDNESDAY 29

THURSDAY 30

FRIDAY 1

Canada Day [Can]

SATURDAY 2

SUNDAY 3

'O proud walls! White towers!
O winged crown and throne of
gold!
O Gondor, Gondor! Shall Men
behold the Silver Tree,
Or West Wind blow again
between the Mountains and the
Sea?'

JULY

S	M	T	W	T	F	S
					1	2
3	4	5	6	7	8	9
10	11	12	13	14	15	16
17	18	19	20	21	22	23
24	25	26	27	28	29	30
31						

July

LEAVES FROM THE BOOK OF MAZARBUL

Black ink, coloured pencil, watercolour

The Book of Mazarbul, found by the Fellowship of the Ring in the Chamber of Mazarbul in Moria, recorded the fortunes of the people of Balin the Dwarf. 'It had been slashed and stabbed and partly burned, and it was so stained with black and other dark marks like old blood that little of it could be read.'

J. R. R. Tolkien intended that these facsimile pages should appear at the beginning of *The Fellowship of the Ring*, Book II, Chapter 5 [The Bridge of Khazad-dûm] but this proved impossible at the time due to the many colours used in their origination.

I

This page of the Book of Mazarbul exemplifies the late form of the Angerthas, called 'the usage of Erebor'. This use would be expected in a kind of diary, written, hastily and without attempt at calligraphy or meticulous consistency of spelling, by Dwarves coming from Dale. Almost all the runes can be interpreted by reference to the section on the Cirth in Appendix E to *The Lord of the Rings*, where also the modifications of the Angerthas Moria made by the Dwarves of Erebor are briefly described.

The Book of Mazarbul was written in Westron, the Common Speech, which in the pages here reproduced is represented, as throughout *The Lord of the Rings*, by Modern English. In writing the Common Speech the Dwarves tended to blend its customary spelling with certain phonetic usages: for they did not like to use any letter or rune in more than one value, nor to express a simple sound by combinations of letters. In representation of this, it will be found that the spelling here is not on the basis of one runic sign for each Modern English letter; for example, the word *chamber* in line 13 is spelt with only five runes, there being a rune for *ch* and a rune for *mb*.

In the transcript that follows these features are not indicated. It may be noted that the word *the* is represented by a short vertical stroke; the word *of* by the rune for *v*; and (often) the word *is* by the rune for *ʒ*. There are also single signs for *ai*, *ay*; *ea*; *ew*; *oa*; *ou*, *ow*. The rune in the top right-hand corner is the numeral 3.

The passage in *The Lord of the Rings* in which Gandalf reads out these pages will be found in *The Fellowship of the Ring*, Book II, at the beginning of Chapter 5, 'The Bridge of Khazad-dûm'. It is possible to make out a little more of the text than Gandalf was able to do in the Chamber of Mazarbul.

1 We drove out orcs from the great gate and guard
2 (r)oom and took the first hall: we slew many in the br
3 (i)ght sun in the dale: Flói was killed by an arr
4 ow. He slew the great chiefta(in) . . . . Flói
5 under grass near Mirrormer(e) . . . . came
6 . . . . ken
7 (w?)e repaire(d) . . . .
8 . . . .
9 We have taken the twentyfirst hall of northen
10 nd to dwell in There is g(oo)d air. . . . .
11 . . . . that can easily be
12 watched . . . . the shaft is clear . . . .
13 Balin has set up his seat in the chamber of Maz
14 arbul . . . . ga(th)ered . . . .
15 gold . . . .
16 . . . .
17 . . . . wonderful (lay?) Durin's Axe . . . . sil
18 ver helm Balin h(a)s ta(k)en them for his own
19 Balin is now lord of Moria:

* * * * * *

20 . . . . today we found truesilver . . . .

21 . . . . wellforged hel(m) . . . .
22 n . . coat m(ade?) all of purest mithril . . . .
23 Óin to seek for the upper armouries of the third deep
24 . . . . go westwards to s . . . . to Hollin gate

* * * *

II

Gandalf paused and set a few leaves aside. 'There are several pages of the same sort, rather hastily written and much damaged,' he said; 'but I can make little of them in this light. Now there must be a number of leaves missing, because they begin to be numbered *five*, the fifth year of the colony, I suppose. Let me see! No, they are too cut and stained; I cannot read them. We might do better in the sunlight. Wait! Here is something: a large bold hand using an Elvish script.'

'That would be Ori's hand,' said Gimli, looking over the wizard's arm. 'He could write well and speedily, and often used the Elvish characters.'

'I fear he had ill tidings to record in a fair hand,' said Gandalf.

The Fellowship of the Ring, Book II,
Ch. 5, 'The Bridge of Khazad-dûm'.

This page is written in the later or Westron convention, in its northern variety, in the application of the Elvish signs to the Common Western Speech. The script can be interpreted from the information given in Appendix E to *The Lord of the Rings*; but the following points may be noted. The vowels are expressed not by *tehtar* but by separate letters, *a*, *e*, *o*, *u* being represented by the *tengwar* 24, 35, 23, 22 respectively (see the table in *The Lord of the Rings*, Appendix E), and *i* by an *i* undotted or with an acute stroke above. For *y*, as in *many* line 9, a *j* is used, and for *w* both *tengwar* 22 and 25; but the diphthongs *ou*, *ow* (as in *sorrow* line 3, *dou(b)t* line 13) and *ew* (as in *slew* line 9) are expressed by a curl over the first element, and *ay* (as in *day* line 4) by two dots over the *a*-letter.

e is often indicated (as in *alone* line 6, *Silverlode* line 10) by a dot placed under the preceding letter.

A bar over a consonant is used to show that it is preceded by a nasal, as in *went* line 6; and a double consonant may be expressed by a bar beneath the latter, as in *barred* line 13. For double *l tengwa* 28 is used.

The runic figure at the bottom of the page is the numeral 5.

1 r ....arz (probably for *ars*, the end of *years*?)

2 since .... ready

3 sorrow .... (y)ester

4 day being the tenth of november

5 Balin lord of Moria fell

6 in Dimrill Dale: he went alone

7 to look in Mirrormere. an orc

8 shot him from behind a stone. we

9 slew the orc but many more ca ....

10 p from east up the Silverlode ....

11 we rescued Balin's b(ody) ....

12 ....re a sharp battle ....

13 we have barred the gates but doubt if

14 ......can hold them long. if there is ....

15 no escape it will be a horrible fate (to)

16 suffer – but I shall hold

III

The last page of the Book of Mazarbul. The runes employed are the same as those on the first of these facsimiles, though the hand is different and the shapes differ in detail. The last line is in the same Elvish alphabet as that used on the second page.

1 We cannot get out: we cannot get out

2 they have taken the bridge and second h

3 (a)ll. Frár & Lóni & Náli fell the

4 re bravely wh(ile the) rest retr ....

5 Ma(zarb)ul. We still ho ....

6 g: but hope u ....n ...... (Ó?)ins p

7 arty went 5 days ago but (today) only

8 4 returned: the pool is up to the wall

9 at Westgate: the watcher in the water too

10 k Óin – we cannot get out: the end com

11 es soon we hear drums drums in the deep

They are coming

I

II

III

 # July

MONDAY 4

Independence Day [USA]

On July 4th S.R. 1418 Boromir set out from Minas Tirith.

....

Weeks 28-29

TUESDAY 5

WEDNESDAY 6

New Moon ●

THURSDAY 7

FRIDAY 8

SATURDAY 9

SUNDAY 10

JULY

S	M	T	W	T	F	S
					1	2
3	4	5	6	7	8	9
10	11	12	13	14	15	16
17	18	19	20	21	22	23
24	25	26	27	28	29	30
31						

July

MONDAY 11

TUESDAY 12

Battle of the Boyne Holiday [NI]

WEDNESDAY 13

THURSDAY 14

First Quarter ◗

FRIDAY 15

SATURDAY 16

SUNDAY 17

JULY

S	M	T	W	T	F	S
					1	2
3	4	5	6	7	8	9
10	11	12	13	14	15	16
17	18	19	20	21	22	23
24	25	26	27	28	29	30
31						

 # July

MONDAY 18

On July 18th S.R. 1419 Éomer returned to Minas Tirith.

Weeks 30-31

TUESDAY 19

WEDNESDAY 20

THURSDAY 21

Full Moon ○

FRIDAY 22

SATURDAY 23

SUNDAY 24

JULY

S	M	T	W	T	F	S
					1	2
3	4	5	6	7	8	9
10	11	12	13	14	15	16
17	18	19	20	21	22	23
24	25	26	27	28	29	30
31						

July

MONDAY 25

TUESDAY 26

WEDNESDAY 27

THURSDAY 28

Last Quarter ◗

FRIDAY 29

The Fellowship of the Ring
first published, 1954

SATURDAY 30

SUNDAY 31

'Search for the Sword that
  was broken:
  In Imladris it dwells;
There shall be counsels taken
  Stronger than Morgul-spells.'

JULY

S	M	T	W	T	F	S
					1	2
3	4	5	6	7	8	9
10	11	12	13	14	15	16
17	18	19	20	21	22	23
24	25	26	27	28	29	30
31						

August

ORTHANC

Pencil, black ink, coloured pencil

In the first manuscript of Book III, Chapter 8 of *The Lord of the Rings*, Orthanc is described as a 'pinnacle of stone' at the centre of a series of chained paths. 'The base of it, and that two hundred feet in height, was a great cone of rock left by the ancient builders and smoothers of the plain, but now upon it rose a tower of masonry, tier on tier, course on course, each drum smaller than the last. It ended short and flat, so that at the top there was a wide space fifty feet across, reached by a stair that came up the middle.' The tower underwent many revisions, both in word and in art, before Tolkien settled on its final appearance.

ORTHANC (1)

August

MONDAY 1

Holiday [Scotland & ROI]

TUESDAY 2

WEDNESDAY 3

THURSDAY 4

Weeks 32-33

FRIDAY 5

New Moon ●

SATURDAY 6

SUNDAY 7

AUGUST

S	M	T	W	T	F	S
	1	2	3	4	5	6
7	8	9	10	11	12	13
14	15	16	17	18	19	20
21	22	23	24	25	26	27
28	29	30	31			

August

MONDAY 8

In a letter to his publisher, Rayner Unwin, dated 8th August 1953, Tolkien suggested the overall title of *The Lord of the Rings* for his great epic, and the volume titles of *The Return of the Shadow*, *The Shadow Lengthens* and *The Return of the King*.

TUESDAY 9

National Women's Day
[South Africa]

WEDNESDAY 10

THURSDAY 11

During August S.R. 1418 all trace of Gollum was lost. It was thought that he had taken refuge in Moria; but when he at last discovered the way to the West-gate he could not get out.

FRIDAY 12

SATURDAY 13

First Quarter ☽

SUNDAY 14

AUGUST

S	M	T	W	T	F	S
		1	2	3	4	5	6
7	8	9	10	11	12	13
14	15	16	17	18	19	20
21	22	23	24	25	26	27
28	29	30	31			

# August

MONDAY 15

TUESDAY 16

WEDNESDAY 17

THURSDAY 18

Weeks 34-35

FRIDAY 19

Full Moon ○

SATURDAY 20

SUNDAY 21

AUGUST

S	M	T	W	T	F	S
	1	2	3	4	5	6
7	8	9	10	11	12	13
14	15	16	17	18	19	20
21	22	23	24	25	26	27
28	29	30	31			

August

MONDAY 22

TUESDAY 23

WEDNESDAY 24

THURSDAY 25

FRIDAY 26

Last Quarter ◑

SATURDAY 27

SUNDAY 28

The first volume of *The Lord of the Rings* was reviewed by C.S. Lewis in *Time and Tide* as "like lightning from a clear sky… heroic romance, gorgeous, eloquent, and unashamed, has suddenly returned."

AUGUST

S	M	T	W	T	F	S
	1	2	3	4	5	6
7	8	9	10	11	12	13
14	15	16	17	18	19	20
21	22	23	24	25	26	27
28	29	30	31			

September

DUNHARROW

Pencil, coloured pencil

Dunharrow, the mountain refuge of the people of Rohan, underwent several changes in Tolkien's mind in the course of writing *The Lord of the Rings*. At first he envisioned a grassy plateau reached by a winding path up a mountain slope, beyond which was a natural rocky amphitheatre and caves in the walls beyond. He sketched its geography twice within the first manuscript of Book V, Chapter 3, written at the end of 1944. Later, as in the drawing shown, he added great standing-stones guarding the path. Eventually he abandoned the caves and made the refuge simply the upland, the Firienfeld. But the lines of stones remained, marking the road which led finally to the Paths of the Dead.

DUNHARROW

August

MONDAY 29

Summer Bank Holiday [UK]

TUESDAY 30

WEDNESDAY 31

THURSDAY 1

Weeks 36-37

FRIDAY 2

SATURDAY 3

New Moon ●

SUNDAY 4

Father's Day [Aus & NZ]

AUGUST

S	M	T	W	T	F	S
	1	2	3	4	5	6
7	8	9	10	11	12	13
14	15	16	17	18	19	20
21	22	23	24	25	26	27
28	29	30	31			

On September 2nd 1973 J.R.R. Tolkien died, at the age of 81.

September

MONDAY 5
Labor Day [USA & Can]

TUESDAY 6

WEDNESDAY 7

THURSDAY 8

FRIDAY 9

SATURDAY 10

SUNDAY 11
First Quarter ◗

'I sit beside the fire and think
of all that I have seen,
of meadow-flowers and butterflies
in summers that have been;'
Bilbo's Song

On 10th September S.R. 1418 Gandalf escaped from Orthanc.

SEPTEMBER						
S	M	T	W	T	F	S
				1	2	3
4	5	6	7	8	9	10
11	12	13	14	15	16	17
18	19	20	21	22	23	24
25	26	27	28	29	30	

September

MONDAY 12	TUESDAY 13	WEDNESDAY 14	THURSDAY 15

The Silmarillion first published, 1977

Weeks 38-39

FRIDAY 16	SATURDAY 17	SUNDAY 18

Full Moon ○

SEPTEMBER

S	M	T	W	T	F	S
				1	2	3
4	5	6	7	8	9	10
11	12	13	14	15	16	17
18	19	20	21	22	23	24
25	26	27	28	29	30	

On 18th September S.R. 1418 the Black Riders crossed the Fords of Isen.

September

MONDAY 19

TUESDAY 20

WEDNESDAY 21

The Hobbit first published, 1937

THURSDAY 22

Autumnal Equinox

22nd September marks the birthdays of both Bilbo and Frodo.

FRIDAY 23

SATURDAY 24

Heritage Day [South Africa]

SUNDAY 25

Last Quarter ◑

On 23rd September S.R. 1418 Frodo left Bag End.

SEPTEMBER

S	M	T	W	T	F	S
				1	2	3
4	5	6	7	8	9	10
11	12	13	14	15	16	17
18	19	20	21	22	23	24
25	26	27	28	29	30	

October

STANBURG OR STEINBORG (MINAS TIRITH)

Pencil, coloured pencil

Tolkien first sketched Minas Tirith in October 1944, to accompany a preliminary description: 'huge "cyclopean" concentric walls – it is in fact a fort and town the size of a small mountain. It has 7 circles with 7 – 6 – 5 – 4 – 3 – 2 – 1 gates before the White Tower is reached.' The drawing shown here began as a more careful rendering of the city, but Tolkien had only begun to fill in the grey of the stonework when he abandoned the attempt, probably because his mental picture had changed. The Minas Tirith of Book V, Chapter 1 of the published *Lord of the Rings*, built upon the 'out-thrust knee' of Mount Mindolluin, had yet to be realized. The handwritten titles are the Old English and Old Norse forms of a name meaning 'Stone-city', and *Steinborg* again in Elvish *tengwar*.

Stanburg

Steinborg

ᚦᛒᚪᚱᚱᛒ

September

MONDAY 26

Weeks 40-41

TUESDAY 27

WEDNESDAY 28

THURSDAY 29

On 29th September S.R. 1418 Frodo reached the Inn at Bree at night.

FRIDAY 30

SATURDAY 1

SUNDAY 2

Unfinished Tales first published, 198

SEPTEMBER

S	M	T	W	T	F	S
				1	2	3
4	5	6	7	8	9	10
11	12	13	14	15	16	17
18	19	20	21	22	23	24
25	26	27	28	29	30	

From a letter to Allen & Unwin dated 30th September 1955:

"When is Vol. III likely now to appear? I shall be murdered if something does not happen soon."

October

MONDAY 3

New Moon 🌑

TUESDAY 4

First Day of Ramadan
Rosh Hashanah

WEDNESDAY 5

THURSDAY 6

On October 6th S.R. 1418 the camp under Weathertop was attacked at night and Frodo was wounded.

---

*'There is an inn, a merry old inn
beneath an old grey hill,
And there they brew a beer so brown
That the Man in the Moon
himself came down one night to
drink his fill.'*

FRIDAY 7

SATURDAY 8

In October 1955 Bernard Levin reviewed *The Return of the King* as *"one of the most remarkable works of literature in our, or any time."*

SUNDAY 9

OCTOBER

S	M	T	W	T	F	S
						1
2	3	4	5	6	7	8
9	10	11	12	13	14	15
16	17	18	19	20	21	22
23	24	25	26	27	28	29
30	31					

# October

MONDAY 10

Columbus Day [USA]
Thanksgiving Day [Can]
First Quarter ◑

Weeks 42-43

TUESDAY 11

WEDNESDAY 12

THURSDAY 13

Yom Kippur

FRIDAY 14

SATURDAY 15

SUNDAY 16

OCTOBER

S	M	T	W	T	F	S
						1
2	3	4	5	6	7	8
9	10	11	12	13	14	15
16	17	18	19	20	21	22
23	24	25	26	27	28	29
30	31					

From a letter to Stanley Unwin dated 15 October 1937:

"I cannot think of anything more to say about hobbits… but I have only too much to say… about the world into which the hobbits intruded."

October

MONDAY 17

Full Moon ○

TUESDAY 18

WEDNESDAY 19

THURSDAY 20

The Return of the King first published, 1955

On 18th October S.R. 1418 Glorfindel found Frodo, cold and wounded, at dusk after the attack at Weathertop.

FRIDAY 21

SATURDAY 22

SUNDAY 23

OCTOBER

S	M	T	W	T	F	S
						1
2	3	4	5	6	7	8
9	10	11	12	13	14	15
16	17	18	19	20	21	22
23	24	25	26	27	28	29
30	31					

 October

MONDAY 24

United Nations Day
Labour Day [NZ]

Weeks 44-45

TUESDAY 25

Last Quarter ◐

The 25th day of October S.R. 1418 marks the date of the Council of Elrond.

WEDNESDAY 26

THURSDAY 27

FRIDAY 28

SATURDAY 29

SUNDAY 30

British Summer Time ends
Daylight Saving Time ends [USA]

OCTOBER

S	M	T	W	T	F	S
						1
2	3	4	5	6	7	8
9	10	11	12	13	14	15
16	17	18	19	20	21	22
23	24	25	26	27	28	29
30	31					

November

MONDAY 31

Hallowe'en
Holiday [ROI]

TUESDAY 1

Diwali
All Saints' Day

WEDNESDAY 2

New Moon ●

THURSDAY 3

Eid-al-Fitr

FRIDAY 4

SATURDAY 5

SUNDAY 6

3rd November S.R. 1419 marks the end of the War of the Ring.

I sit beside the fire and think
  of people long ago,
and people who will see a world
  that I shall never know.
But all the while I sit and think
  of times there were before,
I listen for returning feet
  and voices at the door.

Bilbo's Song

NOVEMBER

S	M	T	W	T	F	S
		1	2	3	4	5
6	7	8	9	10	11	12
13	14	15	16	17	18	19
20	21	22	23	24	25	26
27	28	29	30			

November

SHELOB'S LAIR

Pencil, black ink, red pencil

The way through Cirith Ungol was originally 'a stair and path leading up into the mountains south of the pass . . . and then a tunnel, and then more stairs and then a cleft high above the main pass. . . .' Tolkien drew this conception on a page of an early draft of Book IV, Chapter 8 of *The Lord of the Rings*. The title 'Shelob's Lair', at lower left, was added later: at the time of the manuscript, the great spider that Frodo and Sam encounter in the pass was named 'Ungoliant'.

The text surrounding the sketch takes up from the point where Gollum, having passed through the tunnel with Frodo and Sam and reached the top of the Second Stair, suddenly flees into darkness.

'That's that!' said Sam. Which is expected. But I don't like it. I suppose we are just exactly where he wanted to bring us. Well, let's get moving away or quick as we can. There was the acheas room by mumal ... I've pure wickedness of poor state, ...

... enough, said Frodo. But we couldn't have got even so far without him. So if we ever manage our errand, then Gollum and all his wickedness will be part of the plan.

So far you say, said Sam. Is that so? Well here we are now.

...stand at the crest... mountain range of Ephel Dúath. Yonder, said Frodo, Look! The road opened out now ... went on up, but ... reach. Beyond and ahead there was an ominous glare in the sky; and like a great notch in the mountain wall or cleft was outlined against it so ... On their right the wall of rock fell away and toward ... indeed but it had no brink. Looky darn Frodo saw ...

Frodo went forward now — the last lap — and he exerted all his strength. He felt that if once he could get in the saddle of the pass and look over into the forbidden land he would have accomplished something. Sam followed. He sensed evil all around him. He knew that they had walked into some trap, but what? He had sheathed his sword, but now he drew it or readied it in the ...for a moment, and stooped to pick up his staff with his left hand

November

MONDAY 7	TUESDAY 8	WEDNESDAY 9	THURSDAY 10
		First Quarter ◖	

Weeks 46-47

FRIDAY 11	SATURDAY 12	SUNDAY 13
Veteran's Day [USA]		Remembrance Sunday
The Two Towers first published 1954.		[UK & Commonwealth]

NOVEMBER

S	M	T	W	T	F	S
		1	2	3	4	5
6	7	8	9	10	11	12
13	14	15	16	17	18	19
20	21	22	23	24	25	26
27	28	29	30			

November

MONDAY 14	TUESDAY 15	WEDNESDAY 16	THURSDAY 17
		Full Moon ○	

FRIDAY 18	SATURDAY 19	SUNDAY 20	

NOVEMBER

S	M	T	W	T	F	S
		1	2	3	4	5
6	7	8	9	10	11	12
13	14	15	16	17	18	19
20	21	22	23	24	25	26
27	28	29	30			

November

MONDAY 21

TUESDAY 22

WEDNESDAY 23

Last Quarter ◗

THURSDAY 24

Thanksgiving Day [USA]

Weeks 48-49

FRIDAY 25

SATURDAY 26

SUNDAY 27

NOVEMBER

S	M	T	W	T	F	S
		1	2	3	4	5
6	7	8	9	10	11	12
13	14	15	16	17	18	19
20	21	22	23	24	25	26
27	28	29	30			

December ✦

MONDAY 28

TUESDAY 29

WEDNESDAY 30

St. Andrew's Day [Scotland]

THURSDAY 1

New Moon ●

FRIDAY 2

SATURDAY 3

SUNDAY 4

'Gil-galad was an Elven-king.
Of him the harpers sadly sing:
The last whose realm was fair
  and free
Between the Mountains and the
  Sea.'

The Fall of Gil-galad

DECEMBER

S	M	T	W	T	F	S
				1	2	3
4	5	6	7	8	9	10
11	12	13	14	15	16	17
18	19	20	21	22	23	24
25	26	27	28	29	30	31

December

BARAD-DÛR

Pencil, coloured pencil, black and red ink

Probably the last, and most striking, of Tolkien's finished pictures for *The Lord of the Rings* is a view of Sauron's fortress in Mordor, Barad-dûr, which was drawn some time after October 1944. It is impeccably rendered, and made more foreboding by the glowing red door and upper windows, as if the interior were as fiery as Mount Doom. Even the mortar between the blocks of stones runs red, as if with fire or blood. Only a corner of the fortress is seen, leaving the reader's imagination to build a larger complex. Mount Doom itself can be seen to the left of the tower, very like Frodo's vision of it on Amon Hen in Book II, Chapter 10: 'Fire glowed amid the smoke. Mount Doom was burning, and a great reek rising.'

December

MONDAY 5	TUESDAY 6	WEDNESDAY 7	THURSDAY 8
			First Quarter ◗

Weeks 50-51

	FRIDAY 9	SATURDAY 10	SUNDAY 11

DECEMBER

S	M	T	W	T	F	S
				1	2	3
4	5	6	7	8	9	10
11	12	13	14	15	16	17
18	19	20	21	22	23	24
25	26	27	28	29	30	31

December

MONDAY 12

TUESDAY 13

WEDNESDAY 14

THURSDAY 15

Full Moon ○

FRIDAY 16

Day of Reconciliation
[South Africa]

SATURDAY 17

SUNDAY 18

DECEMBER

S	M	T	W	T	F	S
				1	2	3
4	5	6	7	8	9	10
11	12	13	14	15	16	17
18	19	20	21	22	23	24
25	26	27	28	29	30	31

 # December

MONDAY 19

TUESDAY 20

WEDNESDAY 21
Winter Solstice

THURSDAY 22

Weeks 52-53

FRIDAY 23
Last Quarter ◗

SATURDAY 24

SUNDAY 25
Christmas Day

DECEMBER

S	M	T	W	T	F	S
				1	2	3
4	5	6	7	8	9	10
11	12	13	14	15	16	17
18	19	20	21	22	23	24
25	26	27	28	29	30	31

MONDAY 26

Boxing Day
St. Stephen's Day [ROI]
Hanukkah begins
Day of Good Will [South Africa]

TUESDAY 27

Christmas Day holiday in lieu

WEDNESDAY 28

THURSDAY 29

FRIDAY 30

SATURDAY 31

New Year's Eve
New Moon ●

SUNDAY 1

*'The Road goes ever on
   and on.
Down from the door where
   it began.
Now far ahead the Road
   has gone,
And I must follow, if I can.'*

JANUARY 2006

S	M	T	W	T	F	S
1	2	3	4	5	6	7
8	9	10	11	12	13	14
15	16	17	18	19	20	21
22	23	24	25	26	27	28
29	30	31				

2006

DUST-JACKET DESIGNS

In January 1954 Tolkien was asked by his publisher to suggest a dust-jacket design for *The Lord of the Rings*. He soon produced several sketches for both the first and second volumes. One design for the first, shown here, features the One Ring, surrounded by the Ring inscription in red *tengwar*, and within it the Eye of Sauron. Set in opposition are the Three Rings of Power held by Gandalf, Elrond and Galadriel. The One Ring is also in this design for *The Two Towers*, but now flanked by the towers of Minas Morgul and Orthanc; above flies one of the Nazgûl. Tolkien's design for *The Return of the King* is his most impressive: it features the winged throne and crown of Gondor, the White Tree and Seven Stars, and the monogram and words of Elendil. Above these is the Shadow of Mordor given gigantic human form, its long arm reaching out across the mountains, its clawed hand like the mouth of a hungry beast.

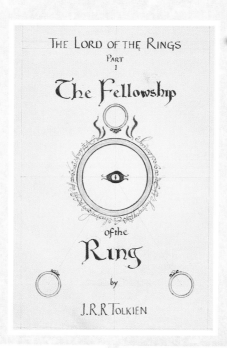

2005

JANUARY

S	M	T	W	T	F	S
						1
2	3	4	5	6	7	8
9	10	11	12	13	14	15
16	17	18	19	20	21	22
23	24	25	26	27	28	29
30	31					

FEBRUARY

S	M	T	W	T	F	S
		1	2	3	4	5
6	7	8	9	10	11	12
13	14	15	16	17	18	19
20	21	22	23	24	25	26
27	28					

MARCH

S	M	T	W	T	F	S
		1	2	3	4	5
6	7	8	9	10	11	12
13	14	15	16	17	18	19
20	21	22	23	24	25	26
27	28	29	30	31		

APRIL

S	M	T	W	T	F	S
					1	2
3	4	5	6	7	8	9
10	11	12	13	14	15	16
17	18	19	20	21	22	23
24	25	26	27	28	29	30

MAY

S	M	T	W	T	F	S
1	2	3	4	5	6	7
8	9	10	11	12	13	14
15	16	17	18	19	20	21
22	23	24	25	26	27	28
29	30	31				

JUNE

S	M	T	W	T	F	S
			1	2	3	4
5	6	7	8	9	10	11
12	13	14	15	16	17	18
19	20	21	22	23	24	25
26	27	28	29	30		

JULY

S	M	T	W	T	F	S
					1	2
3	4	5	6	7	8	9
10	11	12	13	14	15	16
17	18	19	20	21	22	23
24	25	26	27	28	29	30
31						

AUGUST

S	M	T	W	T	F	S
	1	2	3	4	5	6
7	8	9	10	11	12	13
14	15	16	17	18	19	20
21	22	23	24	25	26	27
28	29	30	31			

SEPTEMBER

S	M	T	W	T	F	S
				1	2	3
4	5	6	7	8	9	10
11	12	13	14	15	16	17
18	19	20	21	22	23	24
25	26	27	28	29	30	

OCTOBER

S	M	T	W	T	F	S
						1
2	3	4	5	6	7	8
9	10	11	12	13	14	15
16	17	18	19	20	21	22
23	24	25	26	27	28	29
30	31					

NOVEMBER

S	M	T	W	T	F	S
		1	2	3	4	5
6	7	8	9	10	11	12
13	14	15	16	17	18	19
20	21	22	23	24	25	26
27	28	29	30			

DECEMBER

S	M	T	W	T	F	S
				1	2	3
4	5	6	7	8	9	10
11	12	13	14	15	16	17
18	19	20	21	22	23	24
25	26	27	28	29	30	31